Freedom and Individual Liberty

Anna Maria Mule'

BookLeaf Publishing

India | USA | UK

Presentation by *BookLeaf Publishing*

Web: www.bookleafpub.com

E-mail: info@bookleafpub.com

ISBN: 9789360946746

First edition 2024

*Dedicated to Brendan, Aiden and Beau who
inspire me to do and be better every day*

ACKNOWLEDGEMENT

Grateful

To all the love and support from my wonderful husband, children, and friends and colleagues who encouraged me through difficult times: Darlene Frye, Katarina Vemic, Svetlana Yusupova, Megan Leborious, Rocco Gentile, Regina Constantin Geri Billay, Olga Defilippis and many, many others. My cup is full.

Resistance

Disillusionment wrapped up in a cloud
Of sorrow engulfing my senses and the space
around me
A hazy hue
Sadness at what the world has become
Where wrong is right and right is wrong
A saving grace
A few tweets where the righteous stand up for
themselves
And push past paid protestors blocking a bridge
As they chant for misogyny, child brides, male
superiority, and death to their Aramaic brothers
and sisters in the guise of self determination of
an ancient land
Using words of freedom to hide the new world
order.

Ironic

Ironic is the Racism found in words, not in
children lying on the floor of a cold high school
gymnasium
shelter of their tents
in an old airfield by the ocean
promises not kept

Asylum seekers hide the stench of the cartels
trafficking humans across rivers and fields
providing cheap labor to our anointed
politicians.

The red star over hammer and sickle of
democratic socialism
falls over the fruited plains once overlooked by
the purple majesties of the mountains and our
Hollywood overlords tell us what to think and
see …..

When a net worth of 50 million on a salary of
150k a year earns no rebuke and barely a glance

The vestiges of the founding fathers topple and
our patriotic citizenry cries

Renewal

All the things I want to do and be
when I grow up
and rise anew

Interior designer,
A collector of fine art
A cache of jewelry
To admire and adore
A practical hunter
of discarded goods of sorts
trash to treasure to find

The next Georgia O'Keefe,
An intern for Vera Wang,
A host like Joy Behar

Is it too late to try
Am I finally coming
into myself and blossoming?
The Peace of mind to be as
Beautiful as a flower in bloom
Confidence, humanism,
made in God's image and form
A celebration
and the joy

of ……..

Individualism

Forgetting

It's easier to forget than to remember
All that was
And to look forward into the future
Knowing we will soon forget that as well
Trying to get a glimpse of what is to come and
what is to be
As it moves closer, remains for a moment
And becomes the past
The past was once today and today was once the
future
And the future is yet to be written by the actions
of today

Let it be hopeful and full of joy
Peace instead of misery
Utopia not dystopia
Follow in the footsteps of the good
With integrity

Oppression

Oppression is real
It's exists in our hearts and in our minds
We limit ourselves
By failing to try
By failing to challenge ourselves
By failing to get up and start afresh
Oppression exists in the mind and actions of the
oppressor
look in the mirror
And see … yourself

Sadness

A wave of sadness falls over me
As I drive to work
And a memory arrives to my mind's eye
Reminders of a time and place gone by
A sense of loss and absence
The little griefs amplified over time
A yearning for healing - sweet and bittersweet.
The memories a mix of pain and joy
Of what might and should have been
And what will be

Reflection

Sitting still in the chair
My phone charging beside me
A moment of silence
A profound quiet
An acknowledgement that I got what I wished
for ......

And after all, it was, perhaps,
not what I wanted.
Confused, content, and yet sad
Fulfilled and yet yearning
Brave and somewhat fearful
Courageous to speak and yet still discerning
The longing to have the freedom to let loose
To dismantle what was built
To build again better, bigger and stronger

Courage

What is courage? It is a
welling up of power
Inside within and without
A bravery found in righteous actions
And honest thoughts
A morality from the Book
both the Old and the New
Described succinctly as Good
A manifest of right and wrong
Defined at first glance
In the Garden of Eden
Free will to choose the apple
Free will to follow the path
outlined by omniscience
The omnipotent conscience
Made in the image of the Way
and the Light
Brightening
The heart, the mind, the soul
Choice makes us Human….
Noble… and Divine

Continuum

Not everything is black and white
Much is ensconced in shades of gray
Some orange and bright -
the rising sun in the sky
Some found in the darkening clouds of dusk
But in nuance one can find the value
Placed on the balance scale
Which determines the truth or lie
Or the something in between
The cloudy blending
Of the realities of life
Where perception is reality
And tunnel vision is the norm
Those who can see the shadows
Demonstrate intelligence
indicative of nobility or vice
Depending on the cause

Dissonance

Migrants, asylum seekers, traffic violence,
transportation alternatives, gun violence, school
to prison pipeline
A reframing of reality
To something more palatable
By the communists among us
Who call for collectivism
Environmental Justice
Sustainability
Congestion Pricing
NGO's
They say Tax the Rich written in blood red
On dresses found on the steps of the MetGala
the bridge and tunnel crowd
The basket of deplorables
The red white and blue
The colors of imperialism
By a country the First Lady is ashamed of
The treasonous among us compel
Cancel culture where
Violent protest is freedom of speech and
Nonviolent protest is an insurrection
Brought to you by the organizers in the Senate
To a nation divided
One country tis of thee

Sweet land of misery
A HOUSE DIVIDED
By a complicit media
And untrustworthy puppet strings
Attached to the elite
Predictive programming all the rage
Evil has seeped in
One institution after another

Wealth

Some say that wealth is acquired
Some say it is a condition of inheritance
But of all the human inventions
It is agreeable that Wealth is preferable to want
And for most,
A million dollars would be preferable to none

Ownership

Material items all around us
And we have the illusion of a life well spent
Defined by our possessions
But experiences are often remembered
Shaping who we are and who we become
Our interactions in the world
the impact we wish to see
And our belongings are
a scrapbook of our memories
A history book chronicling our lives

Space

The vastness of space overwhelms
Cognizant of the the inability to understand it's
mystery
What is our human purpose if not to live
But who is watching and why?
The future not yet written can be seen and
foretold
Are we in a Hunger Games of sort
inside a manmade dome?
A simulation of artificial intelligence
If it is imagined it exists
A meta verse of our own making
Acknowledging that
We are energy - neither created nor destroyed
Shape shifting its forms

Atom

Particles in the physical plane
Present all around us
Visible and invisible
The Building Blocks of Matter
Full of force, power, might
Always reactive
Energy moves the earth
And exists in space
A veritable vacuum
Leftovers of the Big Bang
The Makers of everything that matters
In the beginning where God made everything
Out of the darkness and the void
And it was perfection

Love

What is love?
Is it the subtle crashing of the waves on the sand
A dimple in the cheek that appears from a
simple laugh
The innocent smile and glee of a toddler playing
in the sand
A baby's cuddle
A beloved animal waiting at the door to
welcome you home
A caring hand to help you on your way
The joy of happy children
The embrace of a warm home
And the snuggle of your child soon to be too
grown
For a mother's lap

Foreshadowing

Today I went for a walk
Along the promenade of the National Mall
Memorials to the fallen abound
By those who lived the call to freedom
for all
In times of strife and war
A beacon in the storm
The ideals of life, liberty and the pursuit of
happiness
hang in the balance
But our flag still stands in the wind
A lighthouse of hopes
In the ocean
Against the falling iron wall

Leave the world behind

Leave the world behind they say
in 70's chic
And 90's minimalist architecture
With Gotham DC sensibilities
Brooklynites headed east
Escape from Park Slope
Ahem south slope
and former presidents
Predict the coming apocalypse
From Martha's Vineyard
And 5 degrees of Kevin Bacon
Foretell the coming of the civil war
The Lone Star State never ceded
A national identity at stake
Standing in the way of 1984

Deja vu

Is deja vu real or an illusion?
The sense of familiarity
Provoked by a moment
That has already occurred
linear - forward moving
Or does time bend or move backwards
Does time stop
Travel between dimensions
Speeding up and slowing down
depending
On our awareness
Time and space connected
In a vast universe waiting to be explored

Adolescence

Eternal optimism
Vigorous and fresh
Youthful and hopeful
All the years ahead

Boundless energy
Waiting for adulthood
And for the freedom
To be self driven
Enthusiastic and Idealistic
Sensitive to fairness
Vibrant and Sprightly
As Innocent as the angels in heaven
Childish and mature
And wild and full of insight
Awaiting to fully bloom into
The vestiges of adulthood
Exuberance matched only
By the will of a toddler
Youth embodied happiness
Nothing can surpass you

Childhood

Childhood ebbs and flows
The baby year of infancy
The toddler growing into a child
Saying me, me, me and I, I, I
As they toddle behind you trying to do
everything you do

And then the excitement of a child
Playing with friends and running around the
playground
A pure joy
Followed by the pre-teen years of adolescence
And shyness and emotion
Changes that come- both physical and
emotional
And your baby grows into a teen
And now more like you then ever
Maturing into independence
A full fledged member of the family

Be who you are

Be who you are
Be courageous, strong and silly
Virtuous and kind
Petty and angry at times
Be who you are
Smiling and adventurous
True and honest
Simple and plain
And joyful and caring
Be who you are
Passionate and inciteful
When the reason calls for it
Crying when happy or sad
Compassionate and empathetic
Be who you are are
Be yourself
Be your best
It is all that one could want

www.ingramcontent.com/pod-product-compliance
Lightning Source LLC
LaVergne TN
LVHW021358200726
843509LV00014B/2923